The Cusco Theory

COVER

By R. F. Knight

THE CUSCO THEORY

BY R. F. KNIGHT

"Dis-moi ce que tu manges, je te dirai ce que tu es."

[Tell me what you eat and I shall tell you what you are]
-The Origin of the Phrase "You are what you eat"

-Anthelme Brillat-Savarin.

ISBN: 978-0-9917697-0-4

Trademark & Copyright:
© 2012 Knight CAN Press.

Printed in the U.S.A.

A

By R. F. Knight

DEDICATION

This work is dedicated to the countless man hours of the countless scholars who began the insurmountable task of studying these topics before me.

They poured blood, sweat and tears into the research of these subjects, sometimes risking and losing family, friends, positions of prestige and even their lives for the very inception of knowledge into our literature.

To the researchers whom made the task of culminating a plethora of information to be made available to the reader possible, and to the seekers of truth and education on matters of health and society, this work is dedicated to you.

TABLE OF CONTENTS

FOREWORD

Throughout the duration of my corresponding with Righ and the information shared in His thesis.
I would like to extend a quick word of Endorsement and noting what a break-through this not only in my field, but an affirmation of so many of my colleagues works as well. This is astounding information I believe all should read at least once.
-Dr. E. Juwali, ND

I cannot overstate the importance of a healthy diet to my patients.
If the cause of all cultures failing in the past really is because of a poor diet, then you can't afford to eat cheap junk anymore.
I Endorse the Cusco Theory because it makes sense on so many levels.
-Dr. A. Birch, MD

PREFACE

The Purpose of this work is to inspire the minds of Scholars, Doctors and Citizens alike to look at our culture, to challenge our personal beliefs about true health and the history of our food. This is in no way a book of opinion but rather the work of an incumbent of the people with a sole purpose; not to look at relics from antiquity with a sense of wonder, but to deduce evidence and render conclusions based on facts and information just not available to the common man in the decades preceding.

A great deal of effort will be made into explaining and decoding exactly what is being presented in the paragraph before in laymen's terms.

A wise Teacher once told me *"It is best to treat information like a river, dive in head first looking for answers. Sure you may hit your head on a few rocks along the way, but it's not until you take the dive, do you know what is truly at the bottom"*.

I loved that analogy, applying the flow of water to information. As our understanding of the world around us changes, so do our beliefs and way of life. And although issues like Religion, Politics and Race act as stones in the water, never moving on anyone's time. The world will keep on spinning, the information keeps on flowing and in time water erodes rivers into great canyons.

This work is an attempt to change the understanding of Academics about our culture and diet. This work constitutes a strong personal belief that our way of life is under a threat of our own design based upon a single principal; Food.

Please use this as a reference and make up your own mind by doing your own research on the facts, based on the physical evidence of matters.

Hearsay is not Evidence and a pupil is not an expert.

-R. F. Knight

INTRODUCTION

This work has been compiled in response to the pinnacle our society has reached. You could say, we are now at a crossroads. Down one road, we see diversity, prosperity and preservation, down the other, uniformity, conservation and desolation.

Mind you the information provided herein is a sum of many, many facts and years of research, presenting you only with raw data and not much of a 'story' to that effect. Being a Thesis, this work is entitled to the job of proving, through evidence, that a theory is based in logic and reason.

Not only is my own research applied in this work, but that of countless authors on countless papers, articles and published works. The benefit of this fact based narrow view of history, diet and society is by following the trends and behaviors of peoples, cultures and countries respectively, we will see our own future in the past actions of our fathers who fell before us and perhaps will ultimately prove the link between diet & disease.

It is my wish that you allow the logic and reason to speak to you, the facts and information to lead you and the knowledge and wisdom to teach you.

Only by understanding where our food comes from and our ancestral diet, can you begin to see when, where and how our way of life changed.

If you believe; like me, that a strong cognitive constitution and function is in direct relation with proper health. Then surely you can agree that a degree makes no difference in the relation of information, especially to one in application to a degree such as myself.

I wish this work to be considered in your eyes, an open

application to you personally. Despite the constant refute of practical evidence, and the stunning notion that our race may be even older than once thought, but how old and to what level of advancement?

Our desire for knowledge will creep ever deeper into our true history, and nature.

The view of history provided, is intended to outline, mainly, the last 2,000 years and our rise out of the Stone Age, into the Industrial Era and beyond. How our poor diets have affected us in the past and how our synthetic diets are affecting us now. The line to draw would be between Diet and Civilization directly.

Don't take my work for it, let our history do the writing...

By R. F. Knight

OBSERVATION

**CHAPTER ONE:
FOOD, A BRIEF HISTORY**

Before we can discuss civilization and its role in our global issues, we must first understand the very root of our civilizations; Agriculture. Agriculture was developed before civilization; we know this because Humans used to gather in small groups or 'tribes' in order to survive.
In general observation, around 10,000 BCE the Hunter/Gatherer theory where some of the group would go

off picking berries and greens, while others would go hunting for fresh meat was abandoned. Those old ways were traded in for the very first system of planting and growing foods, cultivating animals and their by-products such as milk and skins.

This method spread far and wide as grains grew much faster and filled one up much more than greens or meat. Emmer Wheat was among the first of the grain grown by man. As we consumed the grain, it stimulated us reproductively. The food acted as an aphrodisiac, keeping us full and warm in the winter with oil fires and gave us energy to work in the summer because of the complex starches and sugars. The method spread to Egypt by 7000 BCE and slowly we began to stop wandering the forest and gathering fresh foods to eat. Instead we would eat wheat or other grains that stored well and filled us up.

Farming and husbandry began to make our food options selective, as we would only raise animals that wouldn't escape with ease, such as sheep and goats. Which eventually became Chickens and Cattle and maize was introduced later on by the Olmec and Mayan peoples. Trade routes of the pre-industrial revolution era opened up worldwide grain and seed trading routes like never before. (More notably primitive worldwide trade routes have existed since the 15th century)

As we consumed and stored this grain, it made staying in one area possible. Through this sedentary living we began to build megalithic structures and praying to gods of water and fire. The basic elemental gods and fertility goddesses were a staple of cultures from the beginning of civilization to today.

Civilization came after agriculture that much is certain, but the effects it has played in our evolution and development as a species is yet to be measured.

This Neolithic revolution as it is referred to by scholars, is officially dated to have begun around 8,000 BCE. However some of our earliest stone works including Göbekli tepe date older than 10,000 BCE the current hypothesis where structures were erected by hunters/gatherers, lacks luster based on the simple fact that that food available in the wild and uncultivated nature doesn't provide the quantity of materials available without planting and harvesting of fibers, oils and grains to support the needs of an entire civilization. Even a large group would exhaust the resources in a single area without proper rationing or planned harvesting. With regards to those communal food exchange and sedentary communities; even in material and food rich area's such as prehistoric northern British Columbia, we do not see many megalithic sites dating from a pre Neolithic era. In regards to Mesolithic megaliths such as a tomb or pillars, or monoliths erected in the Mesolithic age. Megalithic structures of such magnitude as Göbekli tepe, Nevalı Çori or more recently (in antiquity) Baalbek in Lebanon (Circ. 9,000 BCE) shows purpose and great masonry work beyond the ability of a small nomadic tribe with only basic flint tool making and hunting capabilities.
Huge ritual sites and living areas aren't uncommon around this era in the area now known as Turkey in the post-Mesolithic times.

Although the Neolithic Revolution is understood as to include an advanced set of agriculture cultivation, irrigation and food storage abilities, the transformation from hunter/gatherer was far more gradual than we would like to believe, with more and more complex structures arising out of the fertile crescent and the middle east around 12,000BP with the ability to sustain large populous and modify the environment to better sustain the civilization.
Small towns and villages now had the ability for high-density population settlements. This included specialized and complex labor diversification, while cultivating a

surplus, as well as the development of non-
portable art, architecture and culture. The first forms of
government such as centralized administrations and
political structures, hierarchical ideologies, and
depersonalized systems of knowledge such as property
regimes and writing. The first example of the
entire Neolithic concept is seen in the Middle
Eastern Sumerian cities (ca. 3,500 BCE) whose emergence
also inaugurates the end of the prehistoric Neolithic period.

In fact many Scholars and Historians give credit to the
Fertile Crescent (Circ. 9000 BCE) being among the first of
cultures to cultivate foods and begin to erect structures.
There are many Neolithic sites dating from 10,000 BP and
beyond, including Göbekli tepe (some inner layers of the
site radio carbon dated at 9500+BP) have had advanced
structures and living areas dating to the 10th Millennia, also
rich with many religious sites and animal relief markings
that have been found in the Fertile Crescent to date.
With this evidence of culture and society arising from
husbandry, the Neolithic revolution in its immediate
definition must be updated from its current dating system
of Cric.10,000 BP – 7,000 BP (8,000 BCE – 5,000 BCE)
to 12,000 BP or the 10th Millennia BCE as the agricultural
revolution began and has been changing ever since this
period. We see evidence of the beginning of primitive and
advanced cultivation of foods and animal husbandry dating
back as far as 15,000 BP in isolated areas. However the
global agriculture revolution as it is understood today
seems to have begun around 12,000 BP.

Although currently no signs of agriculture have been found
in the complex of the structures, we seem to be seeing the
earliest form of deliberate planting and cultivation of
cereals and the hunting of small animals. Such as foxes,

birds and even scorpions. To name a few of the animals carved into stone at the actual structure.

Is it so hard to imagine such advanced capability in small pockets or even wide spread as this new evidence suggests. Belonging to the incipient phase of husbandry, Megalithic structures such as Göbekli Tepe or Nevalı Çori where we are seeing circular megalithic carved orthostats.

Separately; in the Levant, a region in the Eastern Mediterranean there existed a culture although unusual in the fact that it was sedentary or at least semi-sedentary before the introduction of agriculture, the Natufian culture is one of the earliest known examples of hunters/gatherers gaining the ability of advanced food cultivation abilities in the 10th millennium BCE.

"The period is commonly split into two subperiods: Early Natufian (12,500–10,800 BCE) and Late Natufian (10,800–9500 BCE). The Late Natufian most likely occurred in tandem with the Younger Dryas (10,800 to 9500 BCE). In the Levant, there are more than a hundred kinds of cereals, fruits, nuts and other edible parts of plants, and the flora of the Levant during the Natufian period was not the dry, barren, and thorny landscape of today, but parkland and woodland"
-Bar-Yosef, Ofer (1998) (Evolutionary Anthropology 6)

Credited to be the first in the world, referring directly to the work of Dorothy Garrod in her studies of the Shuqba cave in Wadi an-Natuf (in the Palestinian Territories) The Natufian culture lived in the area from roughly 13,000 - 9,700 BCE and shows evidence of deliberately cultivating rye and other cereals and legumes for the purpose of foodstuffs.

Hunting game as large as wild Gazelles, to as small as fish, in fact communal fishing with a large net carried by multiple hunters is seen here as well.

"Additionally deer, aurochs and wild boar were hunted in the steppe zone, as well as onagers and caprids (Ibex). Water fowl

and freshwater fish formed part of the diet in the Jordan River valley. Animal bones from Salibiya I (12,300 – 10,800 BP) have been interpreted as evidence for communal hunts with nets"
As we discover more and more primitive and advanced civilizations dating into antiquity changing our understanding of how our current experience came about, these things shouldn't shock us, nor should we write off discoveries and new information simply because it changes our views.

Even by Humans in our earliest form during the Lower Paleolithic period; Hunting and gathering was employed by Homo erectus some 1.8 million years ago as a survival strategy of small societies for millennia. Even as recent as 0.2 million years by Homo sapiens, while scavenging and gathering slowly became hunting; birds and small animals became a menu item, more nuts, eggs and roots we're gathered as well as fruits such as berries.
Until the transition between the Middle and Upper Paleolithic periods (Circ. 80,000BC – 70,000BC) we lived as small groups living off the land, basic scavenging and food gathering skills. It was at this time hunters began to specialize in game including large animals and select mammals. We began to craft fishing nets and hooks, carve bone harpoons and other tools.
It was during this period that Homo sapiens discovered themselves; they began to become masters of their environments, crafting sharper weapons and making more useful tools, gaining knowledge of the earth's elements such as fire, charcoal and paints.

Our carbon and radiocarbon dating tells us that places like Chauvet caves in southern France and other Aurignacian era findings such as flutes date back to around 32,000 BP (The earliest sample, Gifa 99776 from "zone 10", dates to

32,900±490 BP) If you've never heard of them a brief history on the caves: *"Chauvet-Pont-d'Arc Cave in the Ardèche department of southern France is a cave that contains some of the earliest known cave paintings, as well as other evidence of Upper Paleolithic life. It is located near the commune of Vallon-Pont-d'Arc on a limestone cliff above the former bed of the Ardèche River. Discovered on December 18, 1994"*

This area also contains some amazing pottery, torches and flutes, some of the findings in the Ardèche area date back almost 40,000 years. Amazingly our pottery, flutes, and paintings from that area tell a very simple and true story, that man was the master of his surroundings. Hunting some of the most dangerous creatures known to ever exist and living in some of the harshest conditions our planet could throw at us.

This way of life continued until the end of the Mesolithic period around 10,000 BCE this is why the dating of the Neolithic revolution must be understood as to begin with the start of civilization, as no megalithic structures based on evidence, have been erected by hunters/gatherers without some type of food cultivation ability to sustain the culture. With no regards to monoliths or tombs in the Mesolithic period as a single erection doesn't provide evidence of civilization any more than a primitive round house would. If history wished to equivocate itself forever it would continue to rely on poor data and opinion rather than fact.

Agriculture is a skill that has (evidently) evolved over the last 13,000-15,000 years (BCE) our ability to control the environment around us to better suit our needs, has in turn made us vulnerable to the effects of eating the wrong type of food.

Grains including corn, wheat and barley as well as beans

stored well during harsh weather, and grew easily. We will get to chemically how later; but the foods stimulated us hormonally and physically because of the incompatibility of the complex starches and sugars and our blood and organs.

For hundreds of thousands of years cooking with fire was not a skill we possessed, so eating a few raw red kidney beans often meant certain death.

Our diets consisted mainly of foods that can be easily hunted and/or fished such as small game, carcasses and seafood, and that could be gathered, such as eggs, insects, fruit, seeds, nuts, vegetables, mushrooms and greens.

This is known as the paleolithic diet, and was consumed by man during the paleolithic era for some 2.5 million years and the general belief is that our metabolism and physiology has genetically evolved over millions of years to synthesize only one type of food stuffs; Raw and living foods.

And according to S. Boyd Eaton, *"we are the heirs of inherited characteristics accrued over millions of years; the vast majority of our biochemistry and physiology are tuned to life conditions that existed before the advent of agriculture some 10,000 years ago. Genetically our bodies are virtually the same as they were at the end of the Paleolithic era some 20,000 years ago."*

However our ancestral hominid diet as it is referred to is not only rich in alkaline acids, most of these foods where eaten ground to mouth, meaning that live enzymes, Proteins , minerals and nutrients where present in the food, hence the term 'Living food'. The claim on this diet historically is that we were free from the chronic diseases that come with civilization and/or a synthetic or highly processed diet.

By R. F. Knight

The effort in putting together a small historical view of our diets over the last few thousand years was in an attempt to show you that not only do we inherit a way of life from our ancestors, but by defying it, we are seeing every culture rise and fall because of the wrong food, or conquest of a peoples consuming the wrong foods.

The information in this chapter is meant to enlighten, but not deny the evidence that our race is much older than previously imagined and has been struggling to survive for millennia's, With over 250 underwater cities found to date, and the increasing evidence our race extends vastly beyond our current understanding and our contemporary dating.

The most important thing to take from this chapter is a firm understanding where the evolution of grain cultivation came from; most recently we are seeing people turn away from natural gathering, and trading it in for husbandry and farming. This has allowed us to sustain a large sedentary populous and create the type of living environment today in which we have become accustomed too, but has in turn caused the downfall of every people in antiquity. With this staggering evidence, surely it can be explained chemically? The good news is food has been broken down into a science, literally.

In the next chapter we will take a look at our diet, at disease and ultimately their effects on our Cultures.

Of course this information is pertaining to the end of the last glacial period when the continental ice sheets melted (although still in an ice age known as the 'Pliocene-Quaternary glaciation' this is seen in current continental ice sheets still existing, such as Greenland and the Antarctic) after the global memory of our great 'flood' when the shores rose hundreds of feet because of the frozen water melting and swallowed many cities whole and effectively wiped out much of the evidence and current cultures that existed at that time along those ancient shores. We are only beginning to find the remnants of these ancient societies, so a conclusion on their own food gathering methods whatever they may be is impossible to account on at this time.

This has been the Observation, a look at the history of our food. We know that for hundreds of thousands of years we ate a steady diet of living food, until we began to manipulate our environment and grow grains, cultivate roots and beans to cook. And keep animals for slaughter and ritual purposes.
We have seen our civilization, architecture, culture and way of life explode over the last few thousand years directly linked to our diet.
Perhaps through a better understanding of the human frame can you begin to understand the impact that the wrong food has not only had on our bodies, but on our civilization and more recent, globally.
The phrase *"What you put in your mouth, determines what comes out"* has never been more true in our modern society. Beyond The effects of grain, Synthetic and artificial foods are now a new addition to our palate. Without thousands of years of use to compare it too, we must use the most recent data.

By R. F. Knight

INTRODUCTION

CHAPTER TWO: FOOD IS MEDICINE

More specifically this chapter relates to grains, as an intricate part of our society and religious beliefs. Grains in western society have been included even as the very foundation of the previously suggested 'health food pyramid' as laid out by American Governmental boards. Let us take a look at the effects of grains physiologically before we begin to look at our contemporary civilization and our history lain rich in evident ruin and continual ruin if repeated.

Grains have the power to turn the greatest of populations into obstinate and inimical monsters. But why is this? We have looked at the evidence of grains inception into our diet, we now know when and why we have eaten it. But what is it doing to our bodies? Before we can look at what these substances do to our cultures we must look at the internal damage they are causing.

Biochemically speaking, a Grain, Legume or 'Bean' is designed by nature with harsh anti-nutrients and harmful proteins that cause damage on a cellular level, leading to disease and eventual death.

Even the natural coating on some nut's shells contains arsenic and other toxins.

Any food that requires cooking before consumption is most likely a health hazard waiting to happen, let's look at why;

Grains (and Forage) Legumes contain lectins. Most lectins are non-enzymatic in action and non-immune in origin. Lectins occur ubiquitously in nature. They may also bind to a soluble carbohydrate or to a carbohydrate moiety that is a part of a glycoprotein or glycolipid.

In English this means that Lectins bind to the mucous lining in the intestine (the known cause of many autoimmune diseases).

The proteins in Lectins are Anti-nutrients, meaning that they literally inhibit the absorption of nutrients. Legumes also contain Phytates (including phytic acid) which is known to inhibit important gestational enzymes from doing their jobs (such as pepsin and amylase) and blocking the natural absorption of essential minerals (Calcium, Copper,

Magnesium, etc) Phytates can be found in the bran of grains and some seeds. That is why all seeds must be soaked and allowed to sprout before consumption, as phytates are not digestible in humans (it chelates, making certain micro and macro minerals unabsorbable into the blood stream) by forming insoluble complexes.

It is for this reason I am not condemning rice as its phytic acid also now better known as (IP 6) a natural inhibiter of iron chains, by chelating to the iron molecules this strips tumors and other cells of their iron necessary to function, but phytic acid does not strip the minerals from the organs. That's why it cannot be a large portion of the diet but when used as a supplement or detoxifier it has immense effects. Varying to a degree, and also has anti-oxidant effects. (Although Phytic acid itself is not an anti-nutrient)

Grains such as Wheat and Corn contain Opioid peptides which are known to cause addiction in some people which becomes apparent upon removal from the diet.

Wheat germ agglutinin or WGA is a vitamin D inhibitor and is a known cause of abnormal or premature cell death. Corn is also particularly noted for containing high amounts of starch, insufficient proteins and anti-nutrients.

And is the main source of feed for animals, when fed to cows it causes these adverse effects and more, much faster; Including rickets, as most veterinarians warn against corn and soy feed for animals because of the animals legs breaking whilst trying to stand, it seems the animals weight was insufficient when combined with the calcium stripping Corn/soy feed was leading to brittle and fractured bones.

Peanuts are also a legume, this means that they contain lectins. Just a half cup of peanuts contains almost 11 grams of Omega-6 fatty acids, which is bad for your brain in large quantities (especially) when Omega-3 isn't present. Your Omega-3 Omega-6 intake ratio should be roughly 1:1 in every meal that you consume (a 1:1 ratio is generally recommended). As these acids are available in Blood, Fat and protein (amino acid chains)

Other Forage Legumes include genus such as Alfalfa, Clover and Vetch. Particularly Soy as well, Soy (and almost all other legumes) contain Saponins, These anti-nutrients allow toxins and bacteria to interact with our immune system (cooking them does not destroy the Saponins)

Soy is also unique in a sense that it contains possibly the highest known source of Trypsin inhibitors; trypsin is a digestive enzyme that is necessary for breaking down proteins in the stomach. A lack of Trypsin is a known cause of many digestive and intestinal issues including Diarrhea, bleeding and stomach cramps.

Phytoestrogens act literally as a synthetic estrogen in the human body, along with Goitrogens (an iodine inhibitor) is known to cause damage to the thyroid in women and damage the sexual organs in men.

Soy has many more dangerous properties, but let us continue.

Legumes proteins are incomplete and lack essential amino acids (such as lysine and methionine) remember amino acids are crucial when taking in any type of protein.

Leptin is a 'protein hormone' that plays a key role in regulating energy intake and energy expenditure, including the appetite and metabolism. It is considered to be one of the most important adipose derived hormones.

Leptin also acts on receptors in the hypothalamus of the brain where it inhibits appetite by (1) counteracting the effects of neuropeptide Y (a potent feeding stimulant secreted by cells in the gut and in the hypothalamus); (2) counteracting the effects of anandamide (another potent feeding stimulant that binds to the same receptors as THC), and (3) promoting the synthesis of α-MSH, an appetite suppressant. This appetite inhibition is long-term, in contrast to the rapid inhibition of eating by cholecystokinin (CCK) and the slower suppression of hunger between meals mediated by PYY3-36. The absence of leptin (or its receptor) leads to uncontrolled food intake and eventually resulting in obesity.

What this means, is Grains and Legumes are not only unhealthy, but dangerous to consume. Beyond causing auto-immune diseases (grains are a known cause of 'leaky gut'). In the intestines during digestion, proteins are broken down into amino acids, fats are broken down into fatty acids, and carbohydrates breaks down into usable sugars. When digestion is impeded and the proper chains and acids cannot form and break down to build new tissue. Nothing is supposed to enter the blood stream until it is fully digested. By eating grains, or allowing foreign proteins into the blood stream, (this is the leading cause of all auto immune disorders, including cancer and diabetes). This effects the inner walls of the intestines and holes open up on a cellular level and begin to allow undigested and large proteins into the blood stream. This is the known cause of IBS, Crohn's disease and countless others. When a foreign protein enters the blood, it causes an allergic reaction, (an allergic reaction is an abnormal response to a protein). Leaky gut is also indicated in Alzheimer's and Dementia, through allowing large proteins, such as casein in pasteurized cow milk and more recently; gluten from non-ancestral farming methods (GMO) attach to the brains opiate receptors (Also where Excitotoxins affect) and actually starve the brain. Relating to our culture, societies that include grains (wheat, corn and legumes including soy) as their main protein source and those who drink alcohol are deficient in vitamin B3 or niacin. Some of the symptoms of those who are deficient include: Apathy, depression, anxiety, headaches, etc.

In the consumption of empty calories, we are literally consuming raw energy, with almost 40% of the standard American diet, or (S.A.D) being empty calories in the form of carbohydrates, complex sugars and incomplete proteins combine with an Omega-3/6 ratio of 20:1 we can begin to outline the causality of these substances on our body, immune system, nervous system and brain.

By lowering your bodies (toxic) fat, carb and calorie intake you can lower your leptin levels, naturally, as the intake of empty calories and carbs that leads to an excess of leptin and a leptin resistance that has the same adverse effects as low leptin. Or in English, by eating grains, fried and packaged foods derived of nutrients, minerals, etc.; Leads to an uncontrolled constant feeling of 'hunger' as you are actually not feeding your cells but depleting your body of mineral reserves and making your body (and blood) toxic with excess fatty tissue buildup.

We are seeing an unprecedented amount of data on the effects of these compounds on our cardiovascular systems daily. We can begin to wonder why grain is heralded even in the bible and many other religious texts. To ancient Rome and more recently the staple food of the Americas and Asia and is even the original basis of the American 'Food Pyramid'.

Perhaps oddly enough the Christian Bible even talks about getting a proper sleep and avoiding 'The Bread of Sorrows'.

"They labor in vain that build it: except the L keep the city, the watchman waketh but in vain. It is vain for you to rise up early, to sit up late, to eat the bread of sorrows: for so he giveth his beloved sleep. -Bible (Old Testament)ORDORDPsalms127:1^2).

What I am trying to outline, is the contradiction of the facts and the blatant disregard for evidence of the matter, as we still have healthcare professionals, religious leaders and health guru's recommending whole grains, corn and legumes as part of a daily diet. And we wonder why our culture is so apathetic and degenerating all around us.

Empty Calories are defined as foods that consist mainly of high starch/carbohydrate content that deliver only calories and no real nutritional benefit.

Free radicals are created by toxicity, deficiency and by the normal oxidative process. Deficiency meaning the deficiency of necessary minerals, vitamins, etc and the consumption of processed, starched or foods that are high in glucose (empty calories, etc)

What a free radical is, is an electron that has been removed from its place in an atoms shell, this causes damage to the cells and are arguably the known reason people age (oxidative damage, 'rusting')

These atoms are usually fully formed molecules that give off electrons when they come under these types of stresses, the electrons then fire off from the molecule and attach to other cells beginning the breakdown of that cell.

During the normal oxidative process, about 1,000,000,000 cells are built up, while another 1 Billion are broken down. This is the normal process, however it is through excess environmental, internal and physiological stresses that allows for the continuing formation of the free radicals (e.g. chemical stress (pollution) immune stress (medication or enhanced compounds) and it is through this process that excessive cellular damage occurs.

The cause is as simple as the cure, as harsh compounds enter our body and attempt to wreak havoc and damage cells (this is the known cause of degenerative diseases) The only remedy to halt free radical formation is a natural antioxidant. As antioxidants have the capacity to give off electrons without damaging themselves. This neutralizes the free radicals and promotes a stabilization of the natural oxidative process once again.

Antioxidants are naturally occurring and are completely safe for everyone.

Empty Calories that are known to produce free radicals were originally only a rare addition to our diet (through dates, figs and other natural sources) when consumed with the nutrients stripped in a complex carbohydrate or sugar form, it creates an artificial energy boost that replaces or amalgamates with our natural blood sugars and effects the internal hormone mechanisms that excrete the necessary glucose for the blood.

It is through consumption of this type of food regularly that is a known cause of toxic fat build up and degenerative diseases. A Large quantity intake of empty calories and stimulants (sugar, modified starches, natural energy enhancers) including Coffee's, Energy drinks, Soda's and any food or drink that contains compounds that 'enhance' energy or increase 'vitality' in fact replace natural receptors and insulin/hormone producing elements with artificial stimulants, sugars and excitotoxins.

This state of constant energy expenditure however achieved, continues to go without acknowledgment. And looking at our current definitions; remains undefined.

Restless is a state the dictionary would define as the inability to rest, relax; or one who is never still or always in motion. Restlessness is defined by one who is always fidgeting, Squirming etc.

These terms do not define this serious ailment that in most cases is self-perpetuated but in modern times, we have witnessed even ourselves sitting in chairs full of energy and then when we stand to complete a task our energy suddenly seems to vanish, we are seeing people go to bed full of energy, sleep a full night and wake up feeling like they've barely rested.

We are seeing people from young ages being fed on diets of high starch and empty calorie intake, who grow up with the inability to not only produce their own insulin, but to regulate the bodies energy function without energy enhancements.

It is through the intake of refined sugars, starches and empty calories, that are nutrient deficient. Where 'energy' is replacing vitality and with our receptors being confused until they completely shut down even while in a sedentary state.

Hence, a new term proposed to effectively define this condition that is brought upon oneself through excessive intake of empty calorie, sugars and stimulants to increase energy, through this process a state of 'ir-rest' is achieved, defined only as; A perpetual state of internal restlessness, stagnate and fatigue. (The inability to rest and repose fully) This needn't be defined only as a condition achieved through internal compound stimuli, but rather a multitude of conditional situations that could define it. Such as, when a person goes to sleep at night, the room is supposed to be pitch black and the individual must allow for at least 3 hours of 'preliminary' sleep to achieve all five stages of sleep, the fifth being R.E.M state or 'Rapid Eye Movement'. With modern day high lumen televisions, computers and even the little blinking lights on electronics have been proven enough to disturb one's sleep.

This can also be used as a scientific term explaining states of atomic, quantum and even chemical formulations that (even when stagnate) are in a constant state of internal activity.

In German Irrest is used as a second-person singular subjective to the word 'Irren' Meaning; 'To Wander' (The singular definite, Verb 'Ir' means 'To Go')

So perhaps this new English definition will be grammatically accepted as my explanation to what effects these compounds have on us internally.

By understanding the effects that the foods have on our bodies, we can begin to draw clear lines between diet and society.

By outlining the foundation of western philosophy; but more specifically the western foundation of medicine (distinctly as a discipline onto itself) In the formation and the progression to the modern and future models of healthcare, health and the understanding of disease.

Although the ideals of men are always changing, the evidence remains the same. Although it is sometimes easier to make up a reason to not pursue a topic further, but only by drawing clear lines between history, present and a possible future, can the end thought be truly comprehended or conveyed

"Is it not also true that no physician, in so far as he is a physician, considers or enjoins what is for the physician's interest, but that all seek the good of their patients? For we have agreed that a physician strictly so called, is a ruler of bodies, and not a maker of money, have we not?" – Plato

Plato [Born 424/423 BC] the Greek Philosopher is credited with founding the first Academy of higher learning in the Western world. The reason for us looking at Plato is his accreditation in western learning. Along with his Mentor Socrates, and his student Aristotle, Plato helped to lay the foundations of Western philosophy and science. In Plato's works as well as many other scholars from before and after his time, it was proposed that the most powerful tool that a physician can implore to his (or her) patient is in the care of the human frame. The Platonic Academy the very foundation of western learning understood the strict bond between food and health. Plato often noted the strange names that were given to diseases, Greeks also are famous for calling a people by the food they ate.

Hippocrates [c. 460 BC – c. 370 BC] the Greek Physician is often referred to as the "Father of western medicine" in recognition of his long lasting contributions to the field and as the founder of the Hippocratic School of Medicine. This intellectual school had revolutionized medicine in ancient Greece. Establishing medicine as a discipline, distinct from other fields that it had traditionally been associated with (Such as theurgy and philosophy) and establishing it as a profession.

Hippocrates is credited with being the first person to believe that diseases were caused naturally, not because of superstition and gods. Although different from its original form, the Hippocratic Oath is still taken by many Doctors to date. Hippocrates was credited by the disciples of Pythagoras of allying philosophy and medicine. He also separated the discipline of medicine from religion, believing and arguing that disease was not a punishment inflicted by the gods but rather the product of environmental factors, diet, and living habits.

He is also famously quoted for saying,

"Let thy food be thy medicine".

With this intellectual foundation, the western medical system was undoubtedly destined for success, by defying the established understanding with a more practical, personal approach. The fore fathers of western medicine saw the great link between diet and disease respectively. Unfortunately in our contemporary practice the physician is taught to treat disease. Whether it is a surgeon or pediatrician, all medical doctors practicing in modern times receive less than 30 hours of specific nutrition training.

Should it be a Doctors job to educate the patient about the body and proper care for health? Historically; Yes, however with so much time spent in training on the ability to detect, and diagnose disease and so little spent on the cause and prevention leads to a highly drugged and disease inherit society. The evidence is in the records, public statistics available to anyone who wants them. Heart disease and cancer are the leading killers in the western world. Currently our system has become less ground to mouth (or fresh foods as medicine) to chemical treatments, a pill made from mostly chemical compounds not normally found in nature, so as a result, almost all medication slows the metabolic rate.

Now of course sometimes slowing the metabolic rate can be a good thing, for example if a bee stings you and you have an allergic reaction with your blood and the venom, you would want to slow the metabolic rate. In a regular person, slowing the metabolic rate can mean that cell function is compromised which can lead to further disease and death.

In the last two hundred years we've seemed to discredit natural remedies and natural ways of doing things, simply because the world around us has become more refined, in our minds; so should we. Following suit we have allowed refined agents into our bodies in the assumption that we are doing what we are meant to be doing, surely if we can we must.

It's an assimilation of Western Culture into our behaviours and thoughts, we put institutions in place for the sake of educating and promoting health where as these very institutions are led by disease.

Many of the treatments for modern diseases are pain killers and antibiotics, much like putting a piece of electrical tape over a blinking engine light in a car, the pain killers only stop you from seeing the problem and are not fixing it.

What is disease? Why is it so prevalent in our contemporary society?

Most diseases are now understood to be the body's natural adaptation to abnormalities in order for survival.

Such as high blood pressure could be an adaptation to a diet high in starches, empty calories and poor habit choices including diet, smoking and an unhealthy habitat.

Perhaps the evidence will justify itself:

If you think of the human body almost like a bio machine,

our body rusts because our blood is high in iron, which
breaks down in our cells in a normal cycle. We breathe
oxygen (and nitrogen) (gasses) and send the oxygen
through our blood stream through our lungs with each
breath.
Our blood has a few simple functions; carrying waste from
our cells, transporting oxygen and nutrients to the cells.
Why do we eat, simply because we feel hungry?
Or perhaps we have a desire to feed our cells; like all
mammals Humans consume food on a daily basis. The
purpose of eating is to feed your cells the nutrients and
acids your body uses to regenerate tissue. Consuming the
Amino acids, metals, minerals and nutrients from live plant
matter (especially dark greens and red Vegetables) rich in
alkaline acid is important not only for health but for proper
cellular function.
Plants have evolved (like animals and mammals) over the
millennia to harbor certain elements necessary to their own
survival such as a distinct spice to ward of insects or their
dark or rich colors to promote their own anti-bacterial/cell
feeding enzymes that they require to stay alive.
The act of eating is not only to feed your cells, but to
transfer the properties of one living bio-organism to
another; therefore all food consumption must be looked at
as an important process not to simply fill your gut or excite
your taste buds, but to enrich your body with a transfer of
its natural properties.
Our ancestors looked at the body as a temple, one that
when offered a proper sacrifice, and by worshiping it every
day with ritual, raw food consumption that you were
rewarded in return with a righteous vessel in which to
carry out your holy work.
If you are still thinking of the human body like a machine,
besides breathing a gas and rusting, our stomachs are
conditioned after millions of years of eating raw plants,
vegetation and carcasses that a certain balance of acid must
be retained in order for your human machine to function
properly.
Alkaline acid found in fresh vegetables and some water

sources including fresh coconut is important for protein and nutrient synthesis into proper blood and cellular tissue through the liver.

This is why any chemical medication that doesn't help the blood excrete waste, transport nutrients in the blood stream or help the blood deliver oxygen to the vital organs and brain is dangerous and unnecessary if your stomach acid alkaline ratio is at least 70% fluid content.

Look at the average alkaline battery powered object in modern times, the battery acts as the medium between the energy and desired output. Where the anode (negative terminal) is made of zinc powder, which gives a large surface area for increased current conduction, and the cathode (positive terminal) is composed of manganese dioxide. The alkaline electrolyte is called; potassium hydroxide. Coils then attach to the positive connection and the negative terminal on the battery and power is achieved through chemical reaction.

The human stomach reacts between the two different acids and breaks down the protein, enzymes, minerals, metals and nutrients to transform the matter into energy (and new cells), much like a battery. The wrong type of acid and too much acidity can lead to every disease and illness. (A dead battery)

By creating the proper dilution of alkaline acid/acid base we can properly conduct and transfer the current that the stomach makes.

Isn't it curious that the movement of limbs about the body is called biomechanics?

Bone has been proven to be piezoelectric, meaning that charges of energy can be stored in them; other piezoelectric bio matter would include DNA and many proteins. The word Piezoelectric literally means electricity resulting from pressure, this means that every bone in our body conducts or is conducive to transmitting electricity in response to applied mechanical stress.

Perhaps it is best illustrated by studying of the Electric eel; it is understood that the electric eel has three abdominal pairs of organs that produce electricity: the main organ, the Hunter's organ, and the Sach's organ. These organs make up some four-fifths of its body, and are what give the electric eel the ability to generate two types of electric organ discharges or (EODs): low voltage and high voltage. These organs are made of electrolytes, lined up so that the current flows through them and produces an electrical charge. Chemically speaking, electrolytes are substances that become ions in a solution and acquire the capacity to conduct electricity. Electrolytes are present in the human body, and the balance of the electrolytes in our bodies is essential for the normal function of our cells and our organs. The Interstitial fluid in our bodies is filled with electrolytes and aids our cells and organs especially the kidneys in doing their jobs.

When the eel locates its prey, the brain sends a signal through the nervous system to the electric cells. This opens the ion channel, allowing positively-charged sodium to flow through, reversing the charges momentarily. By causing a sudden difference in voltage, it generates a current. The electric eel generates its characteristic electrical pulse in a manner similar to a battery, in which stacked plates produce an electrical charge. In the electric eel almost 6,000 stacked electro plaques are capable of producing a shock at up to 500 volts.

Now, just using a voltammeter, an athlete's current can be measured at around 2 volts during peak performance. Why is it that our bodies generate a measurable electric current? Perhaps our personal 'biofield' comes from the proper acid and electrolyte solution from stomach content to blood pH?

In fact, electrolytes are important because they are what your cells use to maintain voltages across their cell membranes and to carry electrical impulses (nerve impulses, muscle contractions, etc) across themselves and to other cells. Your kidneys work to keep the electrolyte concentrations in your blood constant despite changes in your body.

Your blood pH is critical not only to health but to life itself, if your blood pH is out of balance by too much, you will die.

Blood pH is regulated to stay within the narrow range of 7.35 to 7.45 (making it alkaline). Blood that has a pH below 7.35 is too acidic. Blood pH, partial pressure of oxygen (pO_2), partial pressure of carbon dioxide (pCO_2), and HCO_3^- (bicarbonate) are carefully regulated by a number of 'homeostatic' mechanisms, which exert their influence principally through the respiratory system and the urinary system in order to control the acid-base balance and respiration, this is measured by an arterial blood gas.

In English that means that when you eat food, your stomach makes hydrochloric acid to break down the food (digesting the proteins and creating amino acid chains). This creates a highly acidic environment, so the chyme (broken down food) then gets passed onto the duodenum where the pancreas secretes bicarbonate to essentially nullify the acidic chyme. Minerals are then taken from the blood to aid in digestion and the transferring of energy and the protein/amino acids chains into new cellular and muscle tissues.

Meaning, Minerals could very well be the most important part of the entire food consumption process (in terms of longevity) from plant to plate these need to be present, cooking your food is guaranteed to destroy most if not all the minerals and phytonutrients in your food (poor storage and transporting foods over long distances also deplete the mineral count in fresh foods).

Beyond Minerals, heating food to above 160° degrees Fahrenheit is recommended as the temperature to kill bacteria in order to consume some foods, and all meats, by heating food to 118° or even this temperature ensures that almost all enzymes, amino acids and minerals will be stripped from the food through the heat transfer. If you're eating meat, this means that the fatty acids, cholesterols, and empty calories are left with the proteins.

Grain fed animals carry almost no minerals in their flesh by the time they reach your plate, cooked or raw. Pellets that farmers give animals as a mineral supplement contain around 10 basic minerals, as humans we need to have an essential 16 minerals known as macrominerals and anywhere between 60 and 90 microminerals (about 17 that we need daily) that our body uses for cell regeneration, bone reconstruction and countless other functions that are aided by minerals. Calcium, Zinc and potassium to a name of few of the essential minerals and need to be consumed through live plant matter for best absorption into the blood stream.

Although over 4,000 Minerals are known to exists, less than 100 are currently understood as viable and only 16 are essential.

The question of how we get extra minerals into our diet can be answered by finding the source of the removal of minerals respectively.

For thousands of years, since the ability to utilize fire as an element, we have been making fires for many reasons (e.g staying warm, cooking, signals, status, etc) After the fire had died down, the next morning often the wood ash would be collected and used on the finger to clean teeth and swab the mouth. (This is still seen by tribes in Africa today; in the morning the wood ash from the previous night's fire is used to brush the teeth). The collected wood ash would be put in the gardens where the foods were growing, and some cultures are noted for cutting their salt with wood ash as salt is normally expensive in small villages. Perhaps unbeknownst to them that wood ash is now known to be a source of minerals and metals essential not only to our bodies, but to the soil in which we grow food in; containing trace elements such as iron, copper, zinc and manganese to name a few, also some heavy metals, aiding in the growing of food by recycling those nutrients back into the soil. Depending on the wood ash's source we see a varying degree of benefit versus problems arising from the metal content, wood ash deacidifies soil by reducing its pH (because of its calcium carbonate content) so it does not contain nitrogen. Wood ash has been an intricate part of our history and yet in January 1882, Thomas Edison's chief electrician turned on the power to the first electric power plant. And before long patents came out one of the first an electric toaster, and stoves, within less than 60 years almost all of North America had traded in wood burning ovens for electric appliances, so an essential part of our diet was removed. The very first patent in the United States Patent office (established in 1790) was for the addition of certain potassium compounds into the wood ash (now pearl or potash) for making soap and fertilizers.

"The doctor of the future will give no medicine, but will interest his patient in the care of the human frame, in a proper diet, and in the cause and prevention of disease".
Thomas A. Edison (1847 – 1931).

Curiously enough that this quote should come from one of the people directly responsible for removing essential minerals (arguably unintentionally) in the first place, although the words ring true today. We are not seeing the evidence based nutrition counselling for modern physicians, nor are we enjoying a disease free lifestyle. Nowadays information is available to us through a multitude of mediums. We see conflicting advice from one expert after the other, from one get skinny in 5 minutes video to another, we are seeing things work for one person but not for the masses, what key element is missing here beyond the next big marketing scheme?

Well, so you understand the importance of fresh foods over processed foods, fruits and veggies over grains, and nuts and seeds over animal flesh, we are going to look at how the body takes in, breaks down and absorbs healthy food into the body.

Although this next part of the chapter is going to be highly technical, understand without knowing how your poor diet is affecting you, you will not know why (or how) to make the right choice when it comes time to sit down to a meal. It is on and with purpose that I attempt to interest you in the care of the human frame, with the maintenance of your human machine and with feeding not only your taste buds, but your cells as well.

Consuming animal flesh as a source of protein or nutrients is not only unneeded, but is harmful to the body.

Animal flesh is highly acidic, when the meat hits the stomach excess nitrogen and uric acid build up and begins to affect the blood pH, calcium is leached from the bones to correct the vital blood pH and buffer the acid. The proteins in cow's milk contain casein a toxic protein to humans, the flesh of the cow is highly acidic and when any food is heated above 118 degrees the enzymes and minerals begin to deplete.

Beyond the calcium wash from the bones, excess calcium can be stored in the kidneys (kidney stones) and passed through urine.

The effect that acid has on the blood, directly relates to Osteotherousus where calcium is being washed through the bones because of a highly acidic environment, in fact a 2001 study shows a great example of this stating:

"Bones are especially affected by blood pH as they tend to be used as a mineral source for pH buffering. Consuming a high ratio of animal protein to vegetable protein is implicated in bone loss in women"

-Sellmeyer DE, Stone KL, Sebastian A, Cummings SR (January 2001).

Again; when the level of calcium in your blood becomes too low, osteoclast activity increases (These C Cells literally strip your bones of Calcium) to try and return this necessary mineral back into your blood stream. CSRs' (Calcium Sensing Receptors) in the parathyroid gland respond with parathyroid hormone (PTH) that stimulates (tremendous) amounts of osteoclast cell activity while provoking other hormonal activity as well.

Cholesterol has been long toted as a 'bad' thing, especially for your heart. However, HDL Cholesterol is the essential ingredient to all hormones, your body uses cholesterol like it uses any other fatty acid that enters your blood, LDL cholesterol is generally seen as a bad thing, which again is necessary in the repair of oxidative damage and LDL

cholesterol is the precursor to stress hormones in the body, and is also technically not cholesterol but a protein carrier. The excess or unused cholesterol is eliminated through bile (and) the digestive tract. HDL cholesterol will actually bind to LDL and bring it back into the liver for storage and use at a later time. Also, if you think your cholesterol may be a little high, soluble fiber helps to lower cholesterol naturally.
The cholesterol our body generates is essential not only in repair of the arterial walls. But acts as a pre-vitamin D in our systems, and is the main ingredient of bile salts.

* * *

The buildup of adipose tissue (fatty tissue) both abdominally and arterially walks hand in hand and has everything to do with in inability to regulate the blood sugar hormones.
As outlined in previous pages, certain food stuffs do inhibit and damage the normal hormonal receptors of the body.
Your body is in a constant state of motion,
even while sleeping your heart beats away & your lungs still need to deliver oxygen to your blood.
By inhibiting your natural perpetual state, you damage your physical body, your peripheral organs and nerves as well.
By further understanding the natural cell ramification processes of the human body, a full view of the cellular damage will be outlined.
Bone Marrow can be viewed as a sort-of blood defense armory, producing platelets to clump together and actually repair blood cells that may become damaged by certain processes both natural and Habitual (Eating, environmental stress, etc)
The platelets are important not only on a cellular level, but for overall health in the long run.
They are responsible for the formation and clotting of blood, an imbalance (too little or too high) can also be a problem.

When we are born, our bone marrow is red and healthy. As we age and as certain loads require more and more of the bone marrow to produce this necessary to life clotting agent; The bone marrow begins to yellow (This is because of fat tissue build up to replace the used marrow)

As this yellowing occurs most often in the long bones of the arms and legs in adults, we can see the severity varying in relation to diet and blood acidity.

The electrical conductivity of the bone also decreases; this not only reduces your ability to regulate the bodies energy, but this yellowing also inhibits and decreases the production of the platelets that can lead to various health problems. Vitamin E and Fish Oils have long been known to increase platelets naturally (and decrease yellow fatty tissue of the bone marrow)

as well as Vitamin K (this is why most children are given a Vitamin K shot shortly after birth) and Calcium.

To be specific, Thrombopoietin is a glycoprotein produced in the liver (parenchymal cells) the kidney's and bone marrow (BM).

(Also known as the megakaryocyte growth and development factor or MGDF)

is responsible for platelet production in bone marrow by actually encouraging the megakaryocytes (BM cells) to fragment into the many tiny platelets.

If the production of THBO (Thrombopoitein) is disrupted, this can also immediately affect platelet production.

It is the platelets that bind to any rough surfaces (to heal worn and damaged cells) however, an excess amount of cholesterol in the blood will actually get stuck to artery walls and on the surface of cell's and begin to form clots, because of the platelet binding to rough cellular surface edges.

In the cellular process, which is; the breaking down and building up of new tissue in the body is the single most important factor to human life and survival. If cellular function is impeded or halted, then cellular degeneration is likely to occur.

This is why the consumption of live foods is so important.

Live Enzymes that aid in digestion and nutrition synthesis are only present in live food, which means the less handling of human hands on a produce product the better! Or even to begin growing your own vegetables to ensure proper mineral and soil PH balance during the growing, and a full yield of nutrients, enzymes, minerals, metals and vitamins come harvest time.

This type of food also helps to feed the nervous system; the nervous system is among the very first cells that begin to form when a new human fetus begins to grow. The health and vitality of these cells depend on a healthy diet.

Our ANS or Autonomic nervous system controls a variety of vital functions of our organs and other functions such as breathing.

To the effort of much research and new instruments in measurement and detection; The ENS or Enteric Nervous system has often been described as 'The Second Brain' where the actual number of neuron counts at around a thousandth to that of the brains, roughly 100,000,000.

We now have an explanation for peoples 'gut feelings' about certain things.

The health and ability of this Gastric nervous system depends entirely on the bio availability of the gut's natural flora.

Most if not all, artificial foods damage the intestines bacterial culture and as aforementioned The consumption of these types of foods on a regular basis is the leading cause of physical degeneration internally and also causes excessive damage to the Nervous systems and peripheral organs.

In the normal Oxidative process (Building up and breaking down of tissues) new tissue is replacing the old nearly every second of your life.

Although the majority of processes do operate automatically, often manual maintenance is required.

In the same way, if you don't brush your hair it will become tangled. If you ingest the improper fuel for your human machine, it too eventually breaks down.

This is also why proper sleep is so crucial, sleep is expensive. You spend about a third of your life sleeping. By getting proper rest you can let your body slow its natural processes and actually begin to build healthy new cells without mechanical stresses (moving around).
There exists, mostly unbeknownst to the laymen, two different types of practising physicians.
The opposing terms, coined as Allopathic and Osteopathic medicine although operating in the same field, are inherently completely different.
While Allopathic or Medical Doctors offer mostly Drugs or Surgery as an option for existing disease management. Osteopathic Doctor's however, focus majorly on preventive care and natural alternatives to chemical medication.
The most effective treatment is the fuel for much heated debate; it is to the individuals' inhibitions and/or spontaneities to choose which is best for themselves and their own situation.
An education on first aid, diet and preventive care is in general opinion, enough to keep any person thriving without the use of any institution.
It seems to come down to the principal in which we seek out treatment and information on our health in the first place.
The average person knows very little about nutrition or the benefits of ingesting whole foods. In the same breath, the person who goes to a restaurant that serves a meal derived of nutrients and minerals because the meal is prepared fast and affordable.
It is the very same person who will later go to a hospital for a 'quick-fix' to treat their physical illness.
My Prognosis is that diagnosis has become an atrocious way of dealing with disease. Only by understanding true health and consuming the proper foods can we begin to progress forward as a people.
Believe it or not disease is completely reversible as long as healthy cells continue to replace dead tissue in the body.
By eating the right diet and through proper physical

activity true health can be achieved, as the proper function of the body and optimal function of the cells would constitute an ease of living, whereas any disruption to the system by misbalancing the blood, acids etc. in the body can lead to a dis-ease of living and eventually an early death.

The point of instructing you on the human frame, our blood acid and our electric conductivity was an attempt at furthering your understanding of the human machine, why we need metals, minerals and acids to balance our system. We breathe a gas that actively 'combusts' within our lungs and brings that gas into our blood stream (much like the engine of a car intakes a gas, to bring to its engine for combustion in order to run). We are a living bio system that requires constant maintenance, if you make this maintenance a part of your daily routine then it assimilates into your schedule. Make time for health, then health will make time for you, in terms of longevity and quality of life.

PRACTICE

CHAPTER THREE: CULTURE

We are going to look at our history of failed activities, at how our diets have allowed us to ignore the current situation, the turmoil we are, have and will be experiencing is a direct result of our inability to recognize the effects our diets, habits and beliefs have in our global situation.

In this chapter we will look at how the phrase 'practice makes perfect' does not apply to bad ideas.

As a culture and a global race we cannot allow mistakes of the past to be set in our future actions; meaning we all play a part in what shape the future will take and perhaps by looking at our mistakes and recognizing the futility of the conflict can we begin to stop the vicious cycle we are stuck in.

This is nothing new; we have seen it all before, failing diet, failing governments, Failing Currencies:

Fiat Currency is a term used to describe a currency or monies of a people that become subject to hyperinflation. Hyperinflation arises when a country (Empire, or peoples) over spends or depletes its money supply (usually during times of War or Social upheaval). Instead of collecting taxes to fund their activities, The Government (King or peoples) requiring more funds, deplete the value of money by printing credits as opposed to accepting resources such as Silver, Gold and Silk on face value; Meaning that a people (Empire or Government) can acquire the services and goods at a 'lower price' by devaluing its currency, such as over issuing credits for gold when the supply of gold is low. This trend dates as far back as ancient Rome to as recent as the contemporary monetary system.

Rome provided one of the first examples of a currency debasement, although that in the first century A.D Rome's money, the Denarius, was made of pure silver. It was Emperor Nero who began to include other metals in the creation of the coins to dilute the precious metal with other cheaper ores.

By 54 A.D the Denarius was around 94% Silver content, the Emperors succeeding Nero also continued to dilute the silver used to make the coinage.

The idea was to gain more wealth through trade and conquest, and give less of your wealth away by using cheaper ores in the creation of the monies.

By 218 A.D the Denarius had been diluted to a silver content of just 43%. And it was Emperor Philip the Arab who diluted the silver content to 0.05% and devalued the currency that led to Rome's eventual collapse.

Some Scholars refer to Rome's conquest as 'The world's longest shopping spree' as their beliefs and lust for conquest lead them to capture fertile farms, fisheries and opened up a trade route to various countries trading foods and goods.

By the end of the roman empire the denarius was as little as 0.02% purity and no longer stored any value or was not given a value as exchange for services and goods.

Somewhat more recently and curiously are the French and German examples of Fiat Currency; where a Dictator (or Emperor) has been able to assume power by issuing a new currency in times of harsh economic downfall.

In the late 18th century the French Government issued a paper money called Assignats. This currency was faulty and not based on any intrinsic value. By 1795 A.D The Assignat was hyper inflated to around 13,000% This allowed Napoleon to seize control of the government and military with his issuance of the Gold Franc, A Currency backed by Gold. This Currency was widely accepted by the people and surrounding ally nations and lasted throughout his reign.

Post-World War I Weimar Germany was one of the greatest periods of hyperinflation that ever existed. The Treaty of Versailles was essentially a financial punishment placed on Germany to make reparations.

The sums of money to be paid by Germany were enormous, to repay this debt they printed paper money, and as a comparison to the U.S one dollar at the time on April 1919; 12 marks. By November 1921 it was 263 marks.

And by December 1923 hyperinflation had raised the ratio to around 4.2 trillion marks, it was said that stacks of the paper Marks were used as kindling in German furnaces during the long winter.

People could barely even afford to buy bread for themselves or food for their animals.

Adolf Hitler and the Nazi regime would often make rounds to beer houses in Pre-World War II offering people free sausages and beers to listen to Hitler's new plans for Germany and his new currency.

It is apparent that during times of economic upheaval, currencies, especially those not backed by resources, become devalued and allow Persons and/or Factions to assume control of the peoples, lands and resources who actually create the wealth in the first place.

We are seeing almost the exact same warning signs that brought about the rise of dictators and emperors many times in the past.

All money systems not backed by actual resources has failed in the past, if we keep eating the same food and making the same political choices as we have always done, we are also doomed to inherit a legacy of failure and misfortune.

With most of the world's current monetary systems not backed by resources, and with deficits and debt beyond the control of those who govern it, time and again has been proven to fail and a matter of when is a question best answered by looking at the past.

Through past events, I believe we can see the similarities to the events that are about to take place, based on the progression of actual events that are happening and that have happened.

Most countries operate on a deficit, where the government borrows funds from a private firm 'a Bank' (or Business) at interest in order to fund its activities. This inherit debt will exist indefinitely until either the monetary system collapses or the firm acquires all the countries consolidated land, properties and resources.

The system of government exists as an established 'go-between' for the people and services for the country. There are some exceptions such as Principalities (Government run by a constitutional Prince) and the Commonwealth where a Constitutional Monarch governs the law under their own House of Commons (and/or) Representatives.

Although no political decisions are said to be made, a hierarchal influence is always written into legislature regardless of this minor agreement.

Most of the world's land has been privatized or consolidated.

And (almost) all of the world's natural forests belong to the U.N under protection and conservation laws.

Through the U.N, the U.S (and the U.S.A) through the financing of governments and militant regimes, have formed an Amalgamated Government long ago.

The countries have been long desegregated and with the land consolidated; much like in the popular board game of (traditional) monopoly you and other players try and buy properties, outwit the other investors/relators to control the entire board.

In reality, the only true winner of the game is the person not playing; the 'banker' holds all the money, properties and even when the last player is left standing whom is it that loans the players money and properties in the first place?

In medieval times the settlers were forced to start paying land taxes and having licenses from the king to do things like teach, farm, practice medicine and operate on lands for landlords.

This system still exists today, put in place by those who financed the kings, most countries will not allow you to operate your business without a license, or practice certain trades without licensing (Medical, marine, construction, vehicles, etc).

Since all land, debts and resources are already owned once created, we can assume that once the land was passed down by kings to land lords for ease of control and licenses were issued so the high society knew whom of the lower class were of what profession and supplying proper taxes back to the kingdom. Such is the case of modern business, where all business is inherit oppression.

Any Company; (a group of people, registered with the power of a single person without personal liability) that charges for a service or product with the intention of making any kind of profit is oppressing the customer to allow them access to the product or service. If we are knowingly taking more from a person then it took to produce, ship and display then we are oppressing that person by perpetuating them to do the same in order to fund their activities.

If everyone charges more than an item or service is worth or takes to perform, it propagates a society where most are left with nothing and some are left with all,

What we are seeing today is a socialist society, highly programmed by the state and their religions.

Although historically the opposite has been true, as holding true to virtues and culture passed down by elders is what keeps the family/social structure strong.

By teaching our children to avoid other cultures, religions and ideologies we are again limiting them to a single world view, whatever ideology it may be.

Are Hollywood/Bollywood productions reflections of society or simply as the term suggests; a program?

And surely if that is understood by directors, then some films not developed by mainstream powerhouse distributers; such as those of independent journalist and directors with a message.

Also, holding true to the stereotype that all movies have a message and are not just mindless jargon, with random content, but the millions of dollars spent to craft a message, point of view or an entertainment piece injected with a certain view (Such as a sympathetic undertones or anti-value comedy).

With socialist programming and hate/racist promoted thinking, this is not only referring to the Americas but on a Global scale with all media.

Most religions inherently teach racism and oppression, even Buddhism defies its own principals by allowing the followers to listen to a hierarchy.

I am by no means an atheist, just attempting to point out the similarities between our beliefs and our actions.

By teaching our children to hate, we are robbing them of looking at the world through fresh eyes. We are perpetuating a single world view that is factually and historically untrue. Some may argue that history and fact is one in the same, which indeed is not the case. True history is known and not written, most of what is written is little of what is known, this is true even in this case.

Many novels can be spent at the cost of arguing whether American writers and intellects are actually (unbeknownst to themselves or not) promoting a socialist or communist world view with their writings while attempting the opposite, quite arguably imperialistic conquest of that of an empire rather than the original peacekeeping ideology (guise?) and American international law/policy. This ideological ancestry that is argued to have failed through antiquity and to this day still encompasses writer's pages.

It all seems to be rooted in a loss of liberty, not just ideological liberty, but in liberty as a value. A basic human principal developed by a sense of chivalry and empathy. Instead, replaced with chary and apathy. Liberty is to laugh in the face of a republic, hierarchy or dangerous groups not senselessly but well equipped both mentally and   armed physically not in a stance of war, no, in an act of valor for individual rights and personal sovereignty.

It is also an observation of the culture both ancestral and contemporary, that world peace. An ideal earth promoted by the youth in 60's antiwar rallies (not developed, but made historically popular).

This has already been attained by the wealthy, if the rich are virtually unaffected by war, even on their home land. As those with the funds to avoid or fund a plan such as war. The wealthy are inherently safe from the conflict through having the necessary monies to refute order to engage (or a draft call, etc)

Only the peoples who pick up the supplied weapons and actually participate in a war are perpetuating it.

This is a historical trend that may well be able to be applied to modern times.

That although the poorest of peoples are often the most

oppressed, in furthering the pain of other peoples by participating in conflict, we inherently cause the future pain and suffering of the next generation who believe in the same principals.

Moreover; a nation, group or person seeking relief of conflict need only to halt obviously thwarted efforts of resolution (whether militant or public refusal) and instead fund the culture of the society. Not simply limited to art and science, but to literature and education on proper values, etc.

For it is only through the building and stabilizing of an economy that will in turn raise the production/consciousness of the peoples enough to eliminate in-fighting and promote economic stabilization.

Through extensive research, not a single term exists regarding 'Social Pronunciation'

Let us define being Socially Pronounced, as the ability of a society to self-regulate and to uplift its peoples through rally or protest, through internal designation, not hierarchal.

The limited ability of the populous challenged against full privilege of authority, elected or dictated.

What type of society would we witness comprised of complete public conformity and non-resistant tendencies?

By R. F. Knight

THESIS

CHAPTER FOUR: THE CUSCO THEORY

Alas we come to the conclusion of matters, the point.
And the point of a Thesis is to prove a Theory, in the final
chapter the link between diet and the failure of cultures
will be proven, in fact; we are seeing the evidence all
around us.
We are now at the height of our Society, as most of the
leading nations of the world (E.g Roman, Inca, Killke, and

American) these societies have lasted about 300 years
(give and take). This is the turning point, where peoples
begin to reject the oppressive ways of the religious and
political leaders as they have miss-managed the resources
and built themselves up, leaving very little for the peoples.
Perhaps some examples of grain fuelled societies failures
in the past will shed some light on this elusive subject.
2000 years ago, Rome was (although still in its infancy)
ready to pillage and terrorize the country sides of all
surrounding nations, forcing the pagans to give up their
god's and lands in exchange to be allowed to continue to
use the lands for the romans and worship the roman god(s).
They seized the farm lands and expanded their empire to
new heights, consuming large quantities of meat and
grains; they continued their conquest for more exotic foods
and richer treasures.

Have you ever made a toast at a wedding? Or at a dinner
on a special occasion?

This is a tradition dating back to ancient Rome; often the
soldiers only had a single cup each, so the soldiers would
eat everything out of their cups. During celebrations, they
would clank their glasses together, often eating with bread
and wine in their goblets, this tradition continues to this
day.

Knowing the effects that animal and incomplete proteins
have on the body, perhaps their apathetic, aggressive
behavior is linked directly to their diet?

Famously roman coliseums were built to house gladiators
who would often fight to the death, or participate in deadly
events including chariot races, and spectacles of strength,
agility and stamina.

Historians time and again question how a society could
gather in such hoards to watch their fellow man compete
against one another and even kill another person. But

perhaps the line to draw would be to that of our own football and competitive fighting stadiums, often men physically brutalize one another in spectacles of strength, agility and stamina. During organized fights in arenas in front of adoring crowds, the favorite to win is often chanted too "kill him". Of course not literally, the meaning of the chant is to knock out the opponent, naturally. But just think about the message we are reflecting to ourselves when we participate in these feats or spectacles (even by viewing).

In roman society the man was exalted above all others, men were expected to be strong and always in the masculine. There was so much food from the crops that were gained by the newly established empire, that men would gorge themselves and then regurgitate the stomachs contents in order to stay thin and lean.

In contrast to the current American model of beauty, where women (especially models and those who work in the contemporary media) are encouraged by the society to be a certain weight and attempt everything from starving themselves and plastic surgery to throwing up a freshly eaten meal to maintain a body image to please the society's views.

This 'Tribalism' Has never ceased as cultures have continued in the footsteps of their forefathers in every step except diet. Whereas the availability of processed or foods derived of nutrients (e.g. Empty Calories, Poor Soil conditions, non-ancestral farming methods, etc.)

With all previous cultures having risen and fallen while consuming grains, ancient Egypt, Rome, Mayan and now even the Americas have consumed Corn, Grains (cereals and wheat's) and Legumes as part of a regular diet.

Corn, a standard ingredient in most dishes from the ancient Olmec and Mayan peoples, eventually became a staple of the entire North American continent.

(Maize was not available anywhere else in the world until this time)

Every culture that has relied on Maize as a food source has collapsed because of the incompatibility of the food stuffs and our bodies.

Our history is all too well written with accounts of the Spanish arrival on the Mayan coasts. Uniquely, the Mayan peoples had pushed the limits of their culture and because of their diets when the final blow came (a drought) it was too much psychologically for the people to handle and they began their obscene rituals and thus ended their reign as the leaders in the area,

but something fundamental shifted between the Spanish arriving and the Free Mason founding of America in 1776 by gentlemen such as George Washington and Benjamin Franklin.

After its introduction by the Olmec's and Mayans, some of the Native Americans that inhabited the Americas also utilized maize as a food source and oddly enough experienced the exact same situation as in Ancient Egypt and the Mayan culture; where we see the entire culture literally walking away from their established civilization, to live in the natural world once again.

Referring directly to the pristine conditions found in some of the archeological sites found in Range Creek rising in the Book Cliffs of Utah, where many undisturbed sites where found from the Fremont Culture.

This culture was found to have literally walked away from their established communities; it appears that after moving their granaries (food storage larders) higher and higher into the cliff sides, was in an effort to keep their food away from thieves or other hungry villagers. The granaries were found to have some maize still inside and aside from some animal bones; it seems that a large percentage of the cultures diet relied on maize and the cultivation of maize. As the weather and living conditions became harsher (the general consensus is that a drought hit the area) and food production was severely affected. Artifacts such as baskets left half weaved, toys and pottery were left as if the whole culture stood up and left the area. Evidence supports that they indeed left the area and headed toward the northwest. It may be safe to assume that the effort in building food storage devices higher and higher up the side of a cliff, to where you had to risk your life to climb up and get the food, was in an attempt at keeping the scarce resources safe and manageable from the obviously hungry population.

It has been determined by observations of the modern day Mayan peoples that their ancestors not only influenced Native Americans with the inception of maize, but actually taught them their planting rituals, such as planting with the moon rising's, etc.

So it is very likely that as the social and harvesting practises reached their pinnacle when the drought hit the area that it was indeed too much for the entire society to bare, so they simply left the area.

As being left on your own often meant certain death, we see not a single trace of any member of the community staying behind.

With a clear line being drawn with the types of foods these peoples were/are eating to the degeneration of their physical bodies and its role in our social issues. Most notably this 'old' idea has its foundations in notably one of the most prestigious of men in the profession of dentistry.

In direct regards to one Dr. Weston A. Price most definitely a brilliant man, having been called the 'Darwin of Nutrition' for his linking of diet directly to degenerative diseases and ultimately their effects on our society.

Taking his role in not only to repair, but in the prevention and cause of what he believed and was vindicated on, was the actual physical degeneration of peoples based on the sole principal of nutrient/mineral deficient foods.

His studies published in his 1939 super work: 'Nutrition and Physical Degeneration', clearly defining the adverse effects that poor food quality has not only on the teeth/mouth but on the body as a whole.

Specifically designating that the Modern American diet (M.A.D) which included flour (grains) sugars, and modern processed vegetable fats where the underlying reason we have degenerative diseases at all.

Dr. Price traveled the world on his quest to prove once and for all that cultures who lived naturally and ate justly in fact did not suffer from the same illness and physical degeneration that he was in-fact witnessing in his daily practice.

As aforementioned, Minerals play a key role in our health and quality of our growing soil.

Dr. Price noted that mineral salts were an important dietary addition (as well as vitamin B)

His work compiled over 15,000 photographs of natural people from lands far away such as the Gaelic fisher people of the Outer Hebrides and Native tribes of British Columbia & many other cultures that included isolated 'primitives'.

Referring to peoples who lived without modernized advancements such as electronics, pavement, or even a system of government: Such as completely nomadic and sedentary tribes from all over the world.

(All of the peoples operated on a hierarchal principal and had a social structure)

He documented thoroughly, every member of the many tribes he came into contact with, the thousands of photo's showing peoples living naturally with fully developed facial features and perfectly straight white teeth.

Knowing what we now know about nutrition it makes sense when Dr Price accounts:

"It should now be clear why isolated primitive people in the Swiss Alps and in the islands off the coast of Scotland maintained a high degree of health and a freedom from tooth decay. It should also be clear, why the modernized people in those areas, lost their immunity to tooth decay. The isolated diets contained several times the amount of water soluble vitamins, and particularly, ten times or more the amount of fat-soluble vitamins".

Historically Humans in every area on the globe partake in the consumption of some animal flesh, usually fish or other sea life/flora complemented by fresh foods rich in minerals and vitamins. This paleolithic diet is still practised by these cultures and is recorded to procure health specifically in bone structure and formation.

Dr. Price noted that there was a distinct difference in what one culture ate compared to another, without getting into specifics we find that whatever type of food was being eaten, It had been chosen for its particular type of vitamin content for a specific occasion such as most nomadic tribes practising the consumption of High Vitamin A content when young adults began to go through hormonal changes and contraception practises, including many tribes going to great lengths to secure Roe fish in order to have healthy babies. (Now known to be one of the highest sources of the Omega-3 fatty acid in fish – Nearly 2300mg in just 3 ½ Oz of this particular fish, when eaten raw)

It was also heavily emphasized in the work that all these cultures from Africa to the orient ate some type of fermented food and almost all their food was eaten raw. This allowed for a plethora of digestive enzymes, Key to maintaining health, and the ability to break down and process the fat soluble vitamin and minerals that were present in the foods.

This research was recorded from Europe and Africa to Asia and even the deep forests of North America.

It seems that cultures who have the limited ability to grow grains, or don't practise the consumption of grains as cereals or breads; actually live longer and enjoy a long life free of physical decay and the diseases that plague the civilized world.

It is understood that since the very beginning of their civilization, the Early Egyptians not only had agriculture but placed bread and grains at the very foundation of their own daily diet.

Mayan's uniquely heralded a certain 'god-like' property to maize (corn) and was featured heavily in their mythology. In fact to save the time of explaining and concluding factually what each culture ate, I have devised the following Summary of the 4 main components of the failed cultures diets:

Egypt:

Cereal/Grain/Breads

Legumes

Beer

Meat

Mayan:

Corn

Legumes

Gourds/Peppers

Meat
N. American:
Corn
Cereal/Grain/Breads
Meat
Beer/Oils
Rome:
Cereal/Grain/Breads
Corn
Wine/Beer/Oils
Meat

Startlingly despite the strong differences in the type of food that 'isolated primitives' consumed from one culture to the next, the similarities always remained Fresh & Raw foods, Fish especially roe and salmon, Sea vegetation and in season fruits, vegetables and roots (including some tubers) year round.
All cultures practised the fermenting of their food stuffs, it is through the process of fermentation that the food begins to break down and transform starches and sugars into carbohydrates and alcohols.
If our diets have historically been to consume one type of food stuffs, eating another type or too much of one type can be not only damaging, but clearly deadly.
Is it as simple as to say that Corn and Grains are the downfall of all great civilizations? Yes.
Is it so simply defined? Unfortunately not, like a strawberry's 'seeds' are actually defined as many tiny little fruits.
(Achene's are the fruit, the seeds are inside)
The destruction of our own cultures has a much more intricate role played by none other than man's lust.

Indeed, it could be argued that our advancements over the millennia are not that of political or social triumph over tyranny, but tyranny's elusive succession into law and thought, that we inherently find better and faster ways of killing ourselves off before any real change can take place and that our march towards peace is actually an endless death toll.

But diet clearly affects our habits, emotions, thoughts and actions. Let it be heralded as truth, that the destruction of a society begins at the plate.

With little evidence to the contrary, this may be the only definitive trend in which all failed society's share in quantity.

This narrow view of history, culture and civilization was meant to magnify the use of foods over that of countless other cultural practises, although all peoples are different, unique and require special attention.

We all require the very same nutrients, minerals and enriching sustenance every day in order to survive and thrive.

With the influence of these poor food stuffs over quality nutrient rich foods on our society is measured now by the not only social degeneration that is apparent all around us, but the actual physical degeneration the majority of the populous is experiencing and are mostly oblivious too.

The observation was intended to introduce you to the concept that our cultures and their habits actually date back much further than most ever thought.

That our historical diet was much different from our ancestral diet and the consequences of ignoring our past mistakes are guaranteed to include future ones.

The Introduction was produced in best possible form to instruct you on what the compounds we ingest on a daily basis are actually doing to our bodies, and inform you on the proper combination of dietary material.

The Practise was to conclude that we all inherit a lifestyle that may or may not include the devastating and debilitating effects of socialist nations foreign and domestic.

That despite rhetoric and propaganda, we all in-fact share the same planet and share particulars of the same idea's, passions and mistrusts.

This final Addition, 'The Theory', is intended to prove the link between diet and the internal destruction of the world's greatest civilizations.

Where undoubtedly the group thought process is ultimately altered by apathetic judgments and public shaming, mainly through gestures, spectacles and impatience.

In conclusion; without a shadow of a doubt, I am convinced that like many health care professionals believe; the links between diet and disease, that diet indeed does completely determine the physical well-being of a person.

And that the corner stone of any civilizations diet that includes corn or bread, has or will collapse because of the generational physical breakdown of the peoples. That will have no choice but to turn away from their civilization or face certain death.

Only by consuming whole foods and a variety of foods every day, can we balance the blood ph and truly feed our cells.

This also translates into the continued thriving of our economy and cultures within our civilizations, if we are all healthy and thriving, how can we have a failed economy?

Should we redefine the goals of our culture to include individual physical well-being?

Do our personal goals for the future include physical betterment?

Heed well your own plan of self-betterment wisely, for it is the true fool that ignores his own wisdom.
No time is wasted in the pursuit of further education, and truly nothing can be taught that isn't willing to be learned. To which avail, I hope you found this work edifying in the least.

By R. F. Knight

CONCLUSION

CHAPTER FIVE: WHY CUSCO?

The city of Cusco; can be spelt Cuzco (IPA: [ˈkuθko] or [ˈkusko]; Quechua: *Qusqu* or *Qosqo*, IPA: [ˈqɔsqɔ]) Lays in southeastern Peru, near the Urubamba Valley of the Andes mountain range. Home to some of the most interesting and amazing structures on the planet. The Killke people lived in this area until the 11th Century B.C where they built many religious sites and a great fortress for defense including the Sacsayhuaman. The Inca (Tawantinsuyu) people arrived and built ontop of the site to expand into a great city and made Cusco the Capital of the Inca Empire from their arrival in the 12th Century until the 16th Century when the Spanish invaded in 1553. (The Spanish also built a church atop the Sacsayhuaman when they settled as well)

Cusco was considered to be 'The Naval of the World' during the height of its civilization. The stone works at Puma Punku still baffle Archeologists to this day.

The city was built in the effigy of a Puma, a sacred animal to the Inca's and many Cultures both Ancient and Contemporary. The Puma is a symbol of strength, courage and power, ancient peoples heralded the Panther as being associated with the sun, having a Solar Vibrancy and it is said that when one begins to think of the puma or panther it means that they are coming into a new phase or higher understanding of themselves and the world around them.

The aboriginal name of the city was Qusqu. Although used in Quechua, its origin has been found in the Aymara language. The word itself originated in the phrase "Qusqu Wanka" ('Rock of the owl')

The Puma being a Spiritual symbol of the people meaning the dawning of a higher personal understanding, and the Owl being an Ancient symbol of wisdom. Perhaps the conclusion to draw from this work is the culmination of the

By R. F. Knight

Owl and the Puma; A higher understanding of the world around you through Education and Wisdom.

Happy Inti Raymi

-R F Knight

The goat who breaks the drum
will pay with his skin"
–Old African Saying

Meaning:
[The trouble-maker turns (His or Her-self)
into the instrument to continue the music]

Written In:
Vancouver, British Columbia, Canada.
Published at 12:12PM on 12.12.12
(December 12, 2012)

Printed in the U.S.A

Fnord

By R. F. Knight

ABOUT THE AUTHOR

Righ Frederick Knight was Born and Currently Lives in the Commonwealth of Tir Righ, More widely known as Vancouver British Columbia, Canada.
Righ is a well versed historian and health advocate, having spent the better part of the (Current) last decade studying health. As more opportunities arise and with the completion of more formal education. He seeks a career in Public Health and informing the public through writings and lectures on the importance of a Raw/Living diet.

FUN FACT

Righ is a Gaelic name meaning: King.
Just like Ri or Ryan, but is not pronounced the same.
Much like you would pronounce Kayleigh or Ashleigh,
Righ is said using the double (long) e sound.
Just like Ashley, Ashlee or Ashleigh.
With the equivalent being; Ree or Righ.

By R. F. Knight

Medical Disclaimer:

No advice given herein is meant to be used as a substitute for medical advice, diagnosis or treatment. The views expressed are solely that of the author based on evidence & science.

Legal Disclaimer:

This book is governed under the laws and by-laws of Canada and was produced with the sole intent of Educating, Entertaining and in an exercise of Freedom of speech. All borrowed Quotes, Materials and References, remain the intellectual property of the Authors and are simply used as professional reference for educational purposes.
All information is available in the public domain and this work should be considered a re-telling of the previous information provided.
All the original information contained herein is intended for Educational, Critique, Entertainment, Reference and Academia purposes only.
Please excuse any incorrect or misleading information, as with all research the scholar is limited to the materials that He/She is provided with, general accounts such as observation is that of opinion (based on facts) naturally.
The health advice in this work is based on that of other health care professionals and their research; always talk to your doctor before stopping any prescription medication.

No part of this work should be used as a basis for any health claims,
But instead should be used as a reference guide for your own research further into the matters and materials provide/outlined.

Reference & Further Research:

Keim N, Stern J, Havel P (1998). "Relation between circulating leptin concentrations and appetite during a prolonged, moderate energy deficit in women".

GreGreen ED, Maffei M, Braden VV, Proenca R, DeSilva U, Zhang Y, Chua SC Jr, Leibel RL, Weissenbach J, Friedman JM (August 1995). "The human obese (OB) gene: RNA expression pattern and mapping on the physical, cytogenetic, and genetic maps of chromosome 7".

Clottes (2003b), p. 33. See also Chauvet (1996), p. 131, for a chronology of dates from various caves. Bahn's foreword and Clottes' epilogue to Chauvet (1996) discuss dating.

"Plato". Encyclopaedia Britannica. 2002.

"Hippocrates". Encyclopaedia Britannica. 2002.

Kaushansky K (2006). "Lineage-specific hematopoietic growth factors". N. Engl. J. Med. 354 (19): 2034–45.

Gershon MD (July 1999). "The enteric nervous system: a second brain". Hosp Pract (Minneap) 34 (7): 31–2, 35–8, 41–2 passim.

"The Slow Birth of Agriculture", Heather Pringle

"Wizard Chemi Shanidar", EMuseum, Minnesota State University

Chauvet, Jean-Marie; Eliette Brunel Deschamps, Christian Hillaire (1996). Dawn of Art: The Chauvet Cave. Paul G. Bahn (Foreword), Jean Clottes (Epilogue). New York: Harry N. Abrams. ISBN 0-8109-3232-6. English translation by Paul G. Bahn from the French edition La Grotte Chauvet.

Clottes, Jean (2003a). Return To Chauvet Cave, Excavating the Birthplace of Art: The First Full Report. Thames & Hudson. pp. 232. ISBN 0-500-51119-5.

Clottes, Jean (2003b). Chauvet Cave: The Art of Earliest Times. Paul G. Bahn (translator). University of Utah Press. ISBN 0-87480-758-1. Translation of La Grotte Chauvet, l'art des origins, Éditions du Seuil, 2001.

Komath SS, Kavitha M, Swamy MJ (March 2006). "Beyond carbohydrate binding: new directions in plant lectin research". Org. Biomol. Chem. 4 (6): 973–88. doi:10.1039/b515446d. PMID 16525538

Brennan AM, Mantzoros CS (June 2006). "Drug Insight: the role of leptin in human physiology and pathophysiology--emerging clinical applications". Nat Clin Pract Endocrinol Metab 2 (6): 318–327. doi:10.1038/ncpendmet0196. PMID 16932309

Dubuc G, Phinney S, Stern J, Havel P (1998). "Changes of serum leptin and endocrine and metabolic parameters after 7 days of energy restriction in men and women". Metab. Clin. Exp. 47 (4): 429–34. doi:10.1016/S0026-0495(98)90055-5. PMID 9550541.

Pratley R, Nicolson M, Bogardus C, Ravussin E (1997). "Plasma leptin responses to fasting in Pima Indians". Am. J. Physiol. 273 (3 Pt 1): E644–9. PMID 9316457.

Weigle D, Duell P, Connor W, Steiner R, Soules M, Kuijper J (1997). "Effect of fasting, refeeding, and dietary fat restriction on plasma leptin levels". J. Clin. Endocrinol. Metab. 82 (2): 561–565. doi:10.1210/jc.82.2.561. PMID 9024254

Nuland, Sherwin B. (1988), Doctors, Knopf, ISBN 0-394-55130-3.

By R. F. Knight

Garrison, Fielding H. (1966), History of Medicine, Philadelphia: W.B. Saunders Company.

"Battery FAQ" at www.powerstream.com

Froese, Rainer, and Daniel Pauly, eds. (2005). "Electrophorus electricus" in FishBase. December 2005 version.

Waugh, Anne; Grant, Allison (2007). "2". Anatomy ans Physiology in Health and Illness (Tenth ed.). Churchill Livingstone Elsevier. pp. 22. ISBN 978-0-443-10102-1.

Acid-Base Regulation and Disorders at Merck Manual of Diagnosis and Therapy Professional Edition

(Please note: In the unlikely event we are missing a citation please contact us via this works website: www.cusco.ca to have it included in current versions)

BACK

www.ingramcontent.com/pod-product-compliance
Lightning Source LLC
Chambersburg PA
CBHW071633040426
42452CB00009B/1610